MARK HARMON

The Biography And Untold Story of His Life, Career, Family Background, Relationships, Challenges, Awards, Philanthropy and Legacy

Evelyn Everlore

Table of Content

Introduction

In the ever-evolving tapestry of the entertainment world, there exist rare and enduring talents, individuals whose names resonate through the annals of history, leaving an indelible mark on the hearts and minds of audiences worldwide. **Mark Harmon**, a name that needs no introduction, stands as a testament to the enduring power of charisma, dedication, and an unyielding commitment to the craft of acting.

In this official biography, we embark on a captivating journey through the life and career of a man who has not only graced our screens but also etched his place in the collective memory of generations. Mark Harmon's significance in the entertainment industry is more than the sum of his roles, more than the lines he's delivered, and the characters he's portrayed. It's a story of resilience, artistic brilliance, and the embodiment of cinematic excellence.

From his early days of aspiring actor to becoming a beloved household name, Mark Harmon has captured the hearts of fans spanning multiple generations. His enduring presence on both the big and small screens has turned moments into memories, and characters into legends.

This biography delves into the life of an actor whose journey is a testament to passion, professionalism, and the profound impact one man can have in the world of entertainment. With a career spanning decades, Mark Harmon's significance is more than a footnote in Hollywood's history; it's a chapter unto itself, and one worth exploring in depth.

Chapter 1

Early Life and Family

Mark Harmon's journey from a sunny childhood in Burbank, California, to becoming a Hollywood icon, is a remarkable tale interwoven with family heritage, dreams, and destiny. Born as the youngest of three siblings, Mark's early years were shaped by the remarkable legacies of his parents, their values, and a natural charisma that would eventually set him on a path to stardom.

Harmon's life began in the vibrant city of Burbank, a place that would lay the foundation for his future endeavors. He was the last addition to the Harmon family, with two older sisters, Kristin and Kelly, who, in their own right, made names for themselves in the world of arts and entertainment. The legacy of the Harmon name had already been written in the stars, and Mark was destined to continue the family tradition.

His parents, however, were luminaries in their own domains. His father, Tom Harmon, was more than just a household name; he was a Heisman Trophy-winning football player and a renowned broadcaster. In the realm of sports, Tom Harmon's name was synonymous with excellence, and his passion for the game left an indelible mark on young Mark.

On the other side of the family tree, Mark's mother, Elyse Knox (née Elsie Lillian Kornbrath), was a multi-talented individual. An actress, model, and artist, Elyse brought an artistic sensibility into the family, something that would later manifest in Mark's own creative endeavors. With such remarkable lineage, it was as if Mark was born to tread the boards of the stage and grace the screens of Hollywood.

Mark also had the privilege of being immersed in a rich cultural tapestry. His maternal grandparents were Austrian immigrants, bringing a touch of European heritage into his American upbringing. It's these diverse cultural influences that would later reflect in Mark's versatile acting repertoire, making him the versatile actor we know today.

As Mark Harmon entered the world, he did so as the final piece in a puzzle of artistic genius and sporting prowess. His early years were steeped in the legacy of his family, and little did anyone know that the boy born in Burbank would grow up to be a beloved figure in the world of entertainment.

This chapter in Mark Harmon's biography explores the roots of his talent, nurtured by the heritage of his family and the cultural influences that shaped his early life. It was this upbringing that would set the stage for a remarkable journey, ultimately leading Mark to become a cherished name in the world of acting.

Chapter 2

Education and Early Career

The journey of Mark Harmon through the corridors of education and his first steps into the dynamic world of the entertainment industry is a captivating narrative of determination, passion, and destiny.

Academic Pursuits

Mark Harmon's path to success had humble beginnings. After graduating from Harvard-Westlake School in 1970, he embarked on a two-year academic adventure that would lay the foundation for his future. These years were spent at Pierce College in Los Angeles, where he pursued an associate degree. It was a period of self-discovery and preparation, setting the stage for the bright future that awaited him.

During his time at Pierce College, Harmon displayed the same unwavering commitment that would later define his acting career. His dedication to his studies and personal growth was evident, marking the first stepping stone on a path that would eventually lead him to stardom.

Choosing the Gridiron Over the Silver Screen

At this point in his life, Mark Harmon stood at a crossroads. He had displayed exceptional talent on the football field during his high school years, and this prowess caught the attention of major college football programs. Offers began pouring in, promising him a future as a professional football player.

One of the most intriguing aspects of Mark Harmon's early journey was his choice between a promising football career and the allure of Hollywood. In 1971, after his second season at Pierce, offers from major football programs arrived, including an enticing proposition from the University of Oklahoma, who had recently finished second in the nation. The Oklahoma Sooners seemed like a gateway to athletic glory. However, Harmon made a decision that surprised many; he chose UCLA.

UCLA was not basking in glory during that time, having struggled through a disappointing 2–7–1 season. The contrast was stark: Oklahoma was riding high, while UCLA was at its nadir. Yet, Mark Harmon's decision to don the blue and gold of the Bruins rather than the crimson and cream of the Sooners was a glimpse into his character. It was a decision based on something deeper than statistics and records; it was a choice fueled by his own vision and determination.

From Quarterback to Stardom

Mark Harmon's tenure at UCLA marked the beginning of a new chapter in his life. He transitioned from a college student with a passion for football to becoming a crucial figure in the world of college sports. As the starting quarterback for the UCLA Bruins in 1972 and 1973, he embarked on a remarkable journey.

One of the most legendary moments in his football career came during his first game as UCLA's quarterback. The team achieved a stunning upset by defeating the two-time defending national champion Nebraska Cornhuskers. This victory, despite being considered a significant underdog, captured the essence of an underdog story, a theme that would resonate throughout his life and career.

His remarkable skills on the field were complemented by his academic excellence. In his senior year, Mark Harmon was honored with the National Football Foundation Award for

All-Round Excellence, highlighting his prowess both on and off the field. It was a testament to his dedication to excelling in all aspects of life.

While Mark Harmon's college football career was marked by success, it's interesting to note that he wasn't selected in the 1974 NFL Draft. This pivotal moment in his life marked a turning point. Instead of pursuing a professional football career, he would soon find himself on a different path, one that would lead him to Hollywood's bright lights.

Graduation and New Horizons

In 1974, Mark Harmon walked across the stage at UCLA, receiving his Bachelor of Arts degree in Communications. His graduation was a moment of pride, not just for himself, but for his family and everyone who had witnessed his journey. He graduated cum laude, a testament to his commitment to both academics and athletics.

Mark Harmon's story is a testament to the possibilities that arise when passion and dedication intersect. His academic achievements and early success in football set the stage for what would become a remarkable career in the entertainment industry. However, this was just the beginning. The next chapter of his life would take him from the football field to the silver screen, where he would become a beloved figure in the world of acting.

Conclusion

Mark Harmon's educational journey and early foray into college football were the building blocks of a remarkable career. These formative years laid the foundation for the Mark Harmon we know today—a talented actor, a dedicated individual, and a man who would leave an indelible mark on the world of entertainment. As we delve deeper into his early career, we will witness the transformation of a young athlete into a Hollywood icon.

Chapter 3

Acting Career Beginnings

Early Roles

After completing his college education, Mark Harmon contemplated pursuing a career in advertising or law, exploring diverse avenues beyond the entertainment world. He initially stepped into the business arena as a merchandising director, but the siren call of acting soon beckoned him to change course. It was a pivotal moment that marked the transition from business to the silver screen.

Mark Harmon's journey through the entertainment industry saw him portraying law enforcement and medical personnel in various roles. His initial exposure to the world of acting came in the form of a commercial for Kellogg's Product 19 cereal, where he shared the screen with his father, Tom Harmon, a longstanding TV spokesman for the product.

Thanks to connections within his family, Mark secured his first acting job in an episode of **"Ozzie's Girls,"** a series connected to his sister Kristin's in-laws, Ozzie Nelson and Harriet Nelson. This marked the beginning of his official acting career.

In the mid-1970s, Mark Harmon made guest appearances in episodes of TV series like **"Adam-12," "Police Woman,"** and **"Emergency!"** He also featured in **"905-Wild,"** a pilot episode for a series about L.A. County Animal Control Officers, although the series itself didn't come to fruition. His association with producer and creator Jack Webb led to a role in "Sam," a short-lived 1978 series centered around an LAPD officer and his K-9 partner. Before this, he received an Emmy nomination for *Outstanding Supporting Actor* in a Miniseries or a Movie for his portrayal of Robert Dunlap in the TV movie "Eleanor and Franklin: The White House Years."

In 1978, he was cast in three episodes of the mini-series "**Centennial**," where he portrayed Captain John MacIntosh, an honorable Union cavalry officer.

The mid- to late-1970s saw Mark Harmon making guest appearances on various TV series, including "**Laverne & Shirley**," "**Delvecchio**," "**The Hardy Boys/Nancy Drew Mysteries.**" He also landed supporting roles in feature films such as "**Comes a Horseman**" (1978) and "**Beyond the Poseidon Adventure**" (1979). In 1979, he secured a co-starring role in the action series "**240-Robert**," where he portrayed Deputy Dwayne Thibideaux. The series revolved around the missions of the Los Angeles County Sheriff's Department Emergency Services Detail but had a short-lived run.

The year 1980 brought Mark Harmon a regular role in the prime time soap opera **"Flamingo Road**," where he played Fielding Carlisle, the husband of Morgan Fairchild's character. Despite initial success, the series was canceled after two seasons. Following this, he joined the cast of "St. Elsewhere" in 1983, playing Dr. Robert Caldwell. His stint on the show lasted for almost three seasons before his character's storyline took a bold step in television history. Robert Caldwell contracted HIV through unprotected intercourse, marking one of the first instances of a major recurring television character being portrayed with the virus.

In the mid-1980s, Mark Harmon also became the spokesperson for Coors Regular beer, featuring in television commercials for the brand.

In 1986, Mark Harmon's career soared to greater heights. He was bestowed with the title of *"Sexiest Man Alive"* by People magazine in January. Shortly after leaving his role in *"St. Elsewhere"* in February, he assumed leading roles in television movies, including "*Prince of Bel Air*," where he co-starred alongside Kirstie Alley, and "*The Deliberate Stranger*," where he depicted the real-life serial killer Ted Bundy. This marked a pivotal period in his career, defined by recognition and impactful performances.

In 1987, Mark Harmon made a brief return to episodic television, with a limited engagement on the series "**Moonlighting**," where he portrayed Cybill Shepherd's love interest, Sam Crawford, for four episodes.

The year 1988 saw him co-starring with Sean Connery and Meg Ryan in the feature film "**The Presidio**." He also appeared opposite Jodie Foster in the film "Stealing Home." Despite his involvement in several high-profile roles, Mark Harmon's film career faced challenges. After the lukewarm reception of his 1989 comedy "**Worth Winning**," he made a return to television, featuring in various television movies.

Mark Harmon's next regular television role emerged as Chicago police detective Dickie Cobb, a character he portrayed for two seasons (1991–1993) on the NBC series **"Reasonable Doubts."**

Mark Harmon's journey through the entertainment industry has been a tale of resilience, adaptability, and a continued pursuit of excellence. As we delve deeper into his career, we will witness the evolution of a talented actor who has left an indelible mark on television and film.

Notable Projects: NCIS

In May 2002, Mark Harmon took on the role of Secret Service special agent Simon Donovan in a four-episode story arc on **"The West Wing."** This portrayal marked a significant milestone in his career, earning him his second Emmy Award nomination exactly 25 years after his first nomination.

It was during his appearance on "The West Wing" that Donald P. Bellisario, the creator of "JAG" and "NCIS," noticed Harmon's talent and invited him to guest star in two episodes of "JAG" in April 2003. This was the moment when Mark Harmon's iconic character, NCIS agent Leroy Jethro Gibbs, was introduced to audiences. This marked the beginning of a long and celebrated tenure in the role.

Starting in September of the same year, Mark Harmon assumed the role of Gibbs in the CBS drama "NCIS." This character portrayal became one of the defining roles of his career, and it earned him six nominations at the *People's Choice Awards*, including a win for *Favorite TV Crime Drama Actor* in 2017.

Throughout his time on "NCIS," Harmon had the opportunity to reunite with three of his former "Chicago Hope" co-stars: Rocky Carroll, Lauren Holly, and Jayne Brook. Since 2008, he also took on the roles of producer and executive producer for the show, contributing to its continued success.

In the fourth episode of the show's nineteenth season, Mark Harmon's character, Gibbs, made his exit as a series regular. This departure was set in motion by the events of the previous season finale, marking a significant transition in the series and in the career of this acclaimed actor.

Chapter 4

Personal Life

Mark Harmon's illustrious career in the entertainment industry is only one facet of his life. Beyond the glitz and glamour of Hollywood, he has a rich and vibrant personal life, filled with meaningful relationships and family bonds. In this chapter, we delve into the personal side of Mark Harmon, exploring his background, relationships, and the values that have guided him.

Mark Harmon's personal life is deeply entwined with his enduring marriage to actress Pam Dawber, a union that began on March 21, 1987. Their love has borne two sons, one of whom made appearances as a young Gibbs in several episodes of "NCIS". The couple consciously maintains a low profile, preferring to keep their family life shielded from the public eye. This choice for privacy underscores their commitment to creating a nurturing and sheltered environment for their children.

Mark Harmon's familial ties are further enriched by his connections to some notable individuals. He is the brother-in-law of the late Ricky Nelson, a beloved singer, and John DeLorean, the renowned car magnate. Additionally, he holds the role of uncle to actress Tracy Nelson and to Matthew and Gunnar Nelson, the talented duo behind the rock band Nelson.

In 1987, Mark Harmon took the significant step of filing for custody of his nephew, Sam, who was the son of his late sister, Kristin. This move was rooted in concerns about Sam's well-being and the belief that his mother was not providing the necessary care. Sam's experiences with his mother painted a challenging picture, as he expressed discomfort with her behavior, mood swings, and her efforts to keep him away from his siblings. Despite these concerns, Mark Harmon ultimately withdrew his custody bid.

Mark Harmon's interests extended to the world of sports. In 1988, he assumed a role as part owner of a minor league baseball team known as the San Bernardino Spirit. The same season witnessed a notable player, Ken Griffey Jr., gracing the team before his meteoric rise to the Seattle Mariners in the major leagues. Harmon utilized the team and their home field, Fiscalini Field, as a backdrop for scenes in a film he was starring in, "Stealing Home."

In 1996, Mark Harmon demonstrated not only his courage but also his innate sense of responsibility. He stepped in as a real-life hero when he rescued a teenage boy involved in a harrowing car accident right outside his Brentwood residence. The driver had managed to escape the vehicle, but the passenger remained trapped in the burning car, facing imminent danger. In a swift and fearless act, Harmon used a sledgehammer from his garage to shatter the car window and extricate the passenger from the engulfing flames. The passenger suffered severe burns but survived the accident, a testament to Mark Harmon's bravery and compassion.

Chapter 5

Philanthropy and Humanitarian Work

Children's Hospital Los Angeles

Mark Harmon's commitment to philanthropy is exemplified by his longstanding association with the Children's Hospital Los Angeles. He has been a steadfast supporter of this renowned institution, which is dedicated to providing world-class pediatric care to children in need. His contributions have included not only financial support but also his valuable time and personal involvement in fundraising efforts.

One of the most significant ways in which Harmon has made a difference is through his participation in the annual **"Play LA"** charity event. This event brings together celebrities, sports figures, and philanthropists to engage in friendly competition, all for the benefit of the Children's Hospital Los Angeles. The funds raised during this event have a direct impact on the hospital's ability to provide critical medical care to children, making a profound difference in their lives.

St. Jude Children's Research Hospital

In addition to his involvement with the Children's Hospital Los Angeles, Mark Harmon has extended his philanthropic reach to the St. Jude Children's Research Hospital. This renowned institution is dedicated to advancing research and providing treatment for pediatric catastrophic diseases, particularly childhood cancer. Harmon's contributions to St. Jude have supported their mission of ensuring that no child is ever turned away due to a family's inability to pay for medical treatment.

Harmon's advocacy for St. Jude includes participating in various awareness and fundraising campaigns. His dedication to this cause is not only a reflection of his compassionate nature but also an acknowledgment of the critical importance of medical research and care for children facing life-threatening illnesses.

Veterans and Service Members

Mark Harmon's commitment to philanthropy extends to his support for veterans and active-duty service members. He has been actively involved in campaigns and initiatives that aim to provide assistance and recognition to those who have served and continue to serve their country.

One notable initiative that Harmon has supported is the "Got Your 6" campaign. This national effort focuses on bridging the civilian-military divide by creating opportunities for veterans and showcasing their talents. By participating in this campaign, Harmon contributes to the broader goal of empowering and integrating veterans into various aspects of society, including the entertainment industry.

The Mark Harmon Terri Hatcher Celebrity Baseball Game

In addition to his involvement with established institutions and campaigns, Mark Harmon has used his influence and resources to create charitable events. One such event is the "Mark Harmon Terri Hatcher Celebrity Baseball Game." This annual charity baseball game brings together celebrities and sports figures to raise funds for a variety of charitable causes.

The event not only serves as a platform for fundraising but also as a source of entertainment for fans and supporters. Mark Harmon's ability to use his passion for baseball and his connections in the entertainment industry to benefit charitable causes underscores his commitment to making a positive impact.

Animal Welfare

Mark Harmon's philanthropic efforts are not limited to human causes. He has also shown deep concern for the welfare of animals. His support for animal welfare organizations reflects his belief in the importance of protecting and caring for all living creatures.

Harmon has been associated with organizations dedicated to rescuing and providing care for animals in need. His support has contributed to the well-being and protection of animals, showcasing his compassionate nature beyond the realm of human causes.

Conclusion

Mark Harmon's philanthropic and humanitarian work serves as a testament to his character and values. His commitment to charitable causes demonstrates his desire to make a positive impact on the lives of others, whether they are children in need of medical care, veterans seeking support, or animals requiring protection. His involvement in various initiatives and campaigns reflects a deep sense of responsibility and a genuine desire to give back to the community. Through his philanthropic endeavors, Harmon not only uses his celebrity status for a greater purpose but also sets an example for others in the industry to use their influence to effect positive change. His legacy extends beyond the entertainment world, making him a role model for both his peers and aspiring philanthropists. Mark Harmon's contributions to these causes serve as a reminder that compassion and generosity have the power to transform lives and create a better world for all.

Chapter 6

Legacy and Impact

Mark Harmon's influence in the entertainment industry goes far beyond his roles on screen. His versatile acting has allowed him to seamlessly transition between different genres, captivating audiences with each performance. Most notably, his portrayal of Leroy Jethro Gibbs in "NCIS" has defined a new standard for crime drama protagonists, embodying dedication, leadership, and unwavering principles.

Harmon's impact extends to his colleagues and co-stars, enriching their careers and elevating their performances. Reuniting with former co-stars from "Chicago Hope" on "NCIS" underscores the enduring connections he's forged in the industry. His collaborative spirit and commitment to creating an environment where actors can shine contribute to project success.

As a respected figure in the entertainment industry, Mark Harmon serves as an inspiration to aspiring actors and storytellers. His journey from a young actor making guest appearances to becoming an icon showcases the power of perseverance and dedication.

Mark Harmon's influence is not limited to acting; his role as a producer and executive producer on "NCIS" allowed him to shape the show's creative direction. His behind-the-scenes contributions highlight his multifaceted capabilities and dedication to delivering high-quality content to audiences.

Awards and accolades, including People magazine's "Sexiest Man Alive" and Emmy Award nominations, celebrate his talent and contributions. These recognitions affirm his impact on the industry and the enduring love of his fans.

Beyond his career, Mark Harmon's legacy is defined by his compassion and philanthropic endeavors. His support for children's hospitals, charities, veterans, and animal welfare organizations showcases his dedication to making a positive impact on the lives of others.

In conclusion, Mark Harmon's legacy and impact on the entertainment industry are multifaceted and enduring. His versatile acting, beloved character, and behind-the-scenes contributions have left an indelible mark on the industry. His influence extends to the next generation of talent, and his philanthropic efforts exemplify the importance of using one's platform for the greater good. Mark Harmon's journey is a testament to the power of talent, dedication, and compassion, illustrating that true success is measured not only by accolades but by the positive change one can effect in the world. His legacy continues to shine brightly, reminding us all of the profound impact one individual can make in the realm of entertainment and beyond.

Conclusion

In conclusion, the life and career of Mark Harmon stand as a testament to the enduring power of talent, dedication, and compassion in the entertainment industry. From his early days as a young actor making guest appearances to becoming a celebrated icon, Harmon's journey has been nothing short of remarkable.

His versatility as an actor has allowed him to seamlessly transition between genres, captivating audiences with each performance. Most notably, his portrayal of Leroy Jethro Gibbs in "NCIS" has redefined the standard for crime drama protagonists, embodying dedication, leadership, and unwavering principles. Gibbs has become a symbol of integrity and has left an indelible mark on popular culture.

Harmon's influence extends beyond his roles on screen to his colleagues and co-stars. His collaborative spirit and commitment to creating an environment where actors can shine have enriched the careers of those around him. Reuniting with former co-stars from "Chicago Hope" on "NCIS" underscores the enduring connections he's forged in the industry.

As a respected figure in the entertainment world, Mark Harmon serves as an inspiration to aspiring actors and storytellers. His journey from a young actor making guest appearances to becoming a celebrated icon showcases the power of perseverance and dedication. He exemplifies that success is not solely measured by accolades but by the positive impact one can make on the world.

Harmon's influence extends to his role as a producer and executive producer on "NCIS." His behind-the-scenes contributions have allowed him to shape the creative direction of the show, delivering high-quality content to audiences.

Awards and accolades have celebrated his talent and contributions, affirming his impact on the industry and the enduring love of his fans.

Beyond his career, Mark Harmon's legacy is defined by his compassion and philanthropic endeavors. His support for children's hospitals, charities, veterans, and animal welfare organizations reflects his dedication to making a positive impact on the lives of others.

Mark Harmon's journey is a testament to the power of talent, dedication, and compassion. His legacy continues to shine brightly, reminding us all of the profound impact one individual can make in the realm of entertainment and beyond. Mark Harmon's life and career serve as an enduring source of inspiration and a reminder of the potential for positive change in the world.

Made in United States
Orlando, FL
30 November 2023

39886698R00024